Godspeak

Poetry, Prayers, Songs, Inspiration, and Dedications

"It's not the wings of the Angel that cause it to fly
but rather the Spirit of God that dwells inside"

LARRY JOSEPH SR.

GODSPEAK
POETRY, PRAYERS, SONGS, INSPIRATION, AND DEDICATIONS

iUniverse books may be ordered through booksellers or by contacting:

iUniverse
1663 Liberty Drive
Bloomington, IN 47403
www.iuniverse.com
1-800-Authors (1-800-288-4677)

ISBN: 978-1-4917-5881-6 (sc)
ISBN: 978-1-4917-5882-3 (e)

Library of Congress Control Number: 2015900648

Print information available on the last page.

iUniverse rev. date: 04/14/2015

To my mother Pearl Joseph (1926 – 1994).

Contents

The Way You Are

God can use you if he wants to
without you changing, just being you.
You are who you are no matter
if you are near or if you are far.
God can use the big and the little,
the short and the tall, he can use
whomever he wants,
anyone at all.

It doesn't matter if you are rich or poor,
God will hear
your knock, and he can open
every door.
Sometimes we envy others who
seem to have fought a good fight.
I know that many of them
cry in the night.
You can't always judge by just what you see
because eyes can fool you and me.
Keep on praying because God will look, and
he will see if your name is written in his book.

Lost and Found

I once was lost, but
now I'm found.
Thank you, Jesus,
for coming down.

You paid a debt
I could not pay.
I praise and worship
you every day.

The love you showed for me
is wider and deeper than any sea.
No one else could bear that cross.
Without your love I would be lost.

I have opened my heart and asked you to come in.
Control my heart and help me to live without sin.
I once was lost, and now I'm found.
Thank you, Jesus, for coming down.

You were chosen to live
and not to die.
Anyone telling you different
is telling a lie.
God knew you from the
foundation of the world.
It has been the same for every
man, woman, boy, and girl.
The path you choose is the one
closest to your heart,
but the way you end can be
different from the way you start.

Let Jesus take control,
and let the Holy Spirit claim your soul.
Then repent from your sinful ways.
God will increase your earthly days.
Your life here on earth will go by fast.
Only what you do for Christ will last.
You were chosen to live, and that is true.
You have a chance to change, so what will you do?
Heaven or hell for all eternity;
I don't know about you, but it's heaven for me.

He Who Is without Sin

If you point fingers and
think that everyone else is wrong,
then you are a sinner too,
so just leave me alone.

You know things always seem different
when you are on the outside, looking in,
but take a closer look at yourself;
you also are living in sin.

Only Jesus walked this earth
and never committed a sin.
Only he can change the condition
that you are currently in.

So stop pointing fingers at others
and playing a role.
Start walking toward the light
and save your soul.

Right Path

Walk the right path, and don't try to hear
what Satan keeps whispering in your ear,
trying to entice you to sell him your soul,
promises of love, money, diamonds, and gold.

You attempt to stay on the straight and narrow path.
It's the best way to avoid God's wrath.
Many have already taken Satan's bait.
Just pray for them and hope it's not too late.

The path of a Christian is difficult to keep,
but everlasting life is what you must seek.
Satan will keep testing you every day with zest;
I will pray that you can pass the test.

Whatever your desire, he will provide it all.
Step off the path and have a ball.
Remember one day you will face God's wrath,
because you let Satan lead you off the right path.

The Light

Why don't you come into the light?
It doesn't matter if it's day or night.
The love of Jesus will illuminate your skin,
and you will know that you made it in.
You spent a long time out in the cold,
never letting Jesus protect your soul.
Satan has run free here on the earth.
His reign got shorter with Jesus's birth.

Come into God's marvelous light.
Then Satan will know he is in for a fight.
God's word is sharper than a two-edged sword.
Satan's arm is too short to fight with the Lord.
You had many struggles along the way.
Now it's time to bow down and pray.
Jesus knows what's in your heart;
he knew all along from your very start.

You will never be forced to let Jesus come in;
he will send you a testimony, maybe from a friend.
They will tell you that sin leads to death, but
Christianity offers peace and amazing rest.

Come into the light, and come today.
It's not the time to be foolish and play.
Time is surely drawing near;
very soon the son of God will appear.

The Cross

When I see a cross
I see Jesus sacrificing for the lost.
It's the purest form of love,
Jesus descending to earth from above.
Christ paid for all of our sins,
fighting against Satan and temptation,
the cross that no one else could bear.
God sent Jesus because he really cares.
Jesus was faultless and sin-free.
He stayed on the Cross just for me.
He could have called angels to bring him down,
but he knew that his soul was heaven bound.
Now we have a cross to bear.
Tell all people from everywhere
Jesus ascended from the Cross
just to save all who were lost.
The cross is a symbol of perfect love.
Jesus sacrificed and ascended like a dove.
He was the sacrificial lamb crucified
for every woman and man he hung and died.

Your Face

Don't turn your face from me,
Lord, your face I long to see.
I know that I failed you every day,
but I have repented in every way.
I'm now free from this horrible sin.
You have changed the condition I was in.
It was hard but I found my way;
I had to read the Bible every day.

I was hooked on sin and the street;
now I bow down at Jesus's feet,
testifying to save a soul.
I want my name written on your roll.
Don't turn your back on me,
Lord, your face I long to see.
I've change my ways now, dear
Lord, please lengthen my days.

A Letter from My Heart

I'm writing this letter and I
don't know where to start,
but I'm writing to you
and it comes from my heart.
Have you ever written a letter
to someone you love.
How your life has been changed
by God high above.
This letter could be for anyone—
brother, sister, daughter, or son.
We all have been hurt in this life;
now it's time to get it right.
Jesus wants us to always forgive
and repent from our sin.
Repentance can change the
circumstance we're in.
Maybe you should first write
a letter to yourself
and save your soul
before somebody else.

Your letter could be short or long—
depends on what you say.
Like the words to
a song,
action speaks louder than words.
It's definitely true.
The action you take
reflects the real you.

So write your letter, and this
is how you start:
I'm writing this letter and
it's coming from my heart.

Adam and Eve

Adam should have followed God's plan,
with dominion over all the land.
At first Adam was in the garden alone;
the Garden of Eden was his home.
Adam named all the animals and plants too.
There was a lot of work for him to do.
God saw that Adam was so alone,
so he made him a woman from his bone.
God made Eve for Adam's helpmate.
The serpent tempted Eve and sealed our fate.
Eve didn't want to follow; she wanted to lead.
The sin she committed started the seed.
Adam gave up his power,
so Eve took his right,
and the world was changed forever
after that very first bite.
If Adam had taken his rightful place,
he could have helped the human race.
Adam could not save the world from sin;
that was for Jesus, who died for all men.

Perfect Love

Just like you love your children,
God loves you too, and he
sent his son, Jesus, to die on the Cross
or eternal life would be forever lost.
Jesus showed agape love;
it was very present when he ascended above.
Love like this we have never seen,
the kind of love that fills your dream.

As the storms of life try to bring you down,
in the arms of Jesus your safety is found.
Battles on the left and battles on the right—
only Jesus can take up your fight.
Jesus said he would keep you, and his word is true;
no one can take Jesus away from you.
How wonderful it is,
perfect love for all who are his.

Stand

Life—it isn't as long as it seems.
Each day brings forth new dreams.
In the space of limited time,
many will be dead or dying.
It's time to take a stand for the Lord.
Fight the battle not with a sword,
but with words from God's book;
open it up and take a look.

People look for a reason for life,
wondering why there is so much strife.
Knowing Jesus suffered as a man
is the reason we must take a stand—
committing no sin and taking a stand,
offering eternal life to every man.
We learn this is the reason for life,
praise and worship taking a stand for Christ.

Everlasting Life

The promise of everlasting life
comes from Jesus, the son,
offered to all who persevere to the end.
Repent and live holy without sin.
Study the Bible and change your life;
it will help you endure all the strife.
Run a good race and fight a good fight.
Don't store up treasure to be stolen in the night.

Jesus deserves praise and glory.
He is the reason for this story.
Jesus gave his life that we might live.
He gave all that he had to give.
Walk with assurance that his word is true.
He wants to walk the streets of gold with you.
Keep his commandments in all that you do.
Everlasting life is his promise to you.

As the moral fabric of our society continues to erode, I'm even more encouraged to do God's will.

There is a need for Christian soldiers who will stand up and testify about the goodness of God—Christians who live in a way that others will see God's light and emulate God's lifestyle. In these last days, with so many worldly sins, stay the course on which God set you, and when tribulation comes, you will be able to withstand Satan. Do not listen to Satan's call. Do not accept the mark of the beast and risk eternal damnation.

Drug abuse, sexual perversions, alcoholism, and domestic abuse are all indications of a fractured society. America has succumbed to temptations, leading to the downward spiral of a free and once-great nation rooted in Christianity.

Technology has been a great addition for the betterment of society, but it also has ushered in evil. You can access anything that you desire from your home. Computers tempt you with the things you have a passion for under the veil of secrecy. Advertisements provide visuals, including seductive women or men, homosexuality, and child abuse, but you can't hide from God; he will see your transgressions.

Just like in Noah's time, God is calling on his faithful servants to stand up against a satanic ruled world. He is calling on you to stand up for righteousness. Stand up and have trust that God's word won't come back void and that evil will not last, but Jesus will prevail and his reign will be everlasting! Stand up, Christians.

Prayer in Time of Hopelessness

Lord, I come to you because you are my rock and I know that you are able to deliver me from the pit of despair. I'm not seeing a way out of my iniquity, my pain, my failures. Only through repentance do I have hope, so now, Lord, I have repented from my sins and want you to dwell in my heart. Come, Lord Jesus, and turn my defeat into victory. Fill me with a righteous heart so that there is less of me and more of you. Father, I declare victory right now in the mighty name of Jesus. Amen.

Prayer for Reconciliation

Lord, I have been burdened in my spirit for a long time because of my failure to reconcile with those with whom I have been at odds. Your word says "to be reconciled with your brother first." I'm committing right now to follow your word. Help me. I pray to do your will in all things. In the mighty name of Jesus, amen.

Prayer When Living in Sin

Lord Jesus, have mercy on me, a lowly sinner who is not worthy of your blessings. I have now repented and ask you to blot out my transgressions. Deliver me from all evil and the snares that Satan has laid out before me, and purge my soul from all sin. Lord Jesus, tear down the walls of envy and deceit, and provide me with a clean heart, and I will worship you all my days. In Jesus's name, amen.

Prayer of Appreciation

Thank you, Lord, for all the times you have stood in the gap for me when I was downtrodden and sick. Lord, you died on the Cross for my sins and gave me a chance to have everlasting life, and I praise your name. Help me. I pray to live in a way that is acceptable in your sight. Lord, I pray that my family and friends also live in a way that is acceptable to you. I pray for all who live in darkness to come out into your marvelous light. Amen.

Prayer for Strength

Father, I pray that you will strengthen me where I'm weak and build my faith in your holy word so that I may stand against all evil. Help me, Lord, and give me the strength to remain steadfast in my faith. I have faith that your word will save my soul from eternal damnation. In Jesus's name, I pray. Amen.

Morning Prayer

Lord, I'm blessed that you allow me to rise and see the light of another day that you have created. All praise and glory belong to you. Help me this day, Lord Jesus, to bring a ray of hope in someone's life through word or deed, and I will give you the praise. Keep me on the path of righteousness so that I may glorify you. Make me an instrument for uplifting your kingdom. Amen.

Prayer for Family

Lord, bless my family and keep them in your amazing grace. May the hearts of those who are not walking with you be softened and receptive to your words. Lord, I know the temptations are many, and Satan has led many astray, but you, God, are a mighty shield and can assure victory over all enemies. Grant each person the ability to understand that the wage of sin is death but living by your word is everlasting life. I pray for your blessings in the precious name of Jesus. Amen.

Rapture

I read late one night about
Christians who will one day vanish out of sight.
They will be changed in a moment,
while the rest will be left behind for atonement.
I believe it to be true, and I don't want to be
left behind, so here is what I plan to do:
I'm dedicating my life to you,
working on my salvation,
waiting on the rapture. Oh, yes, waiting on the rapture

Chorus:
When will the rapture come so I can meet the son?
I'm waiting on the rapture. Oh, yes, waiting on the rapture.
All those who remain will be in a grievous time
and accept that Jesus holds back his hand.
Life would then be over for every man.
You must have a rebirth, because it will
be terrible left behind here on earth.
The rapture is going to come.
Many will be caught up in the sky;
others will be left to die.
I'm waiting on the rapture. Oh, yes, waiting on the rapture.

We Love You

Hear the praise as we lift you up daily.
Your holy work we love to do, as we
dedicate our life to only you.
Agape love we freely give to everyone,
singing praises for the glory of the son,
living by the word and telling the true story.
Jesus, you deserve all the praise and glory.

Chorus:
We love you. Yes, we love you.
Wonderful Jesus, we love you.
You are mighty, Holy Father.
Alpha and omega you are.
Omnipresent and heaven is your home.
I know I'll never be alone.
Jehovah, we love you. I tell everyone.
I see that you delivered me and I'm free.
You stayed on that Cross and died for me.
We love you. Yes, we love you.
Wonderful Jesus, we love you.

In a Moment

In a moment with the trumpet sound,
the sky will open up
and Christ will be earthbound—
died on Calvary just for you and me,
died to set souls free.
In a moment, I'll be going home
to kneel at Christ's throne.

Chorus:
No man knows the day or hour when
Christ will return,
returning to the land
with all power in his hand.
In a moment the dead in Christ will rise
up from the grave to meet him in the skies—
died on Calvary just for you and me.
He died to set souls free. In a moment
I'll be going home to kneel at Jesus's throne.

Jesus Has My Back

I know for a fact
that Jesus has my back.
When Satan starts to attack,
Jesus has my back.
He died on the Cross
just to save the lost.
Are you tired of sin,
the condition that you're in?
There is another way:
come to Christ today.
Jesus has my back.
Jesus has my back.
Breaking the law,
you know it's not right.
That's the reason you
can't sleep at night.
If you are tired of sin,
your own situation,
you must be born again.
That's why I know for a fact
that Jesus has my back.

Always Choose Love

No matter what your eyes see or your ears hear,
always choose love and never fear.
Emotions can lead you astray,
but choose love each and every day.
You may have looked for love in a ring;
it's mostly in the lyrics that artists sing.
It is desired all over the world,
more valuable than silver, diamonds, and gold.
People often look for love in the wrong place,
and many ideas of love are a disgrace.
Love can be young, or it can be old.
You have to choose love to save your soul.
When you choose to love Jesus
you must open your heart,
invite him to come in,
then make a new start.

A story that started on the African continent,
where callous, hateful men were sent,
sailing around the Cape slave ships would go,
filling their ships with human cargo.
Ancestors were tortured, and many were killed
just because they resisted the slavers' will,
enslaved in a land they did not know,
working for free while being hated so,
not being able to read or write,
barely speaking English but toiling through the night.
Even though the future looked dim,
they knew that God would not abandon them.
No matter how long they suffered in pain,
one day they would be free again.
It took a strong people to hold to that dream.
Back in Africa some had been kings and queens.
Slaves built this country from the sweat off their backs.
Without slaves America wouldn't be the world leader,
and that is an absolute fact.

Freedom at Last

How many must die?
How many must cry?
People still praying for freedom
like it's going to fall out of the sky.
We have the power
to really make a change,
but politicians always lie, and
life just stays the same.
How long will it take for us to understand
what the constitution
demands?

Nubian Queen

You are the Nubian queen,
appearing in all my dreams.
I appreciate the pain and suffering
that you endured throughout history.
As a man I can hardly imagine how
much pain you suffered, sometimes dying
bringing children into a brutal slave system—
a system that tore your children from your bosom,
a bosom that even nourished the slave master's children.
After their mother's milk had dried,
you were commanded to nurse their babies.
You, my queen, were born from royalty,
as you are a priceless treasure, loved
and respected, as God made you from my own
bone as my helpmate.
I vow to never demean you with derogatory slurs
or raise my hand to you in anger,
for to do so will only lessen
my own manhood, and I love you.

Never Give Up on Love

Never give up on love and
it won't give up on you.
You will have problems,
but love will see you through.

If you walk away from love too soon
your heart may end up in misery and ruin.
Love is a real treasure and hard to find.
If you have patience you can ease your mind.

True love most often doesn't come fast.
If you let God guide you, it will last.
Let him select one he has seen from above,
then pursue her and never give up on love.
Never give up on love,
and it won't give up on you.
Remember that Jesus is love,
and he never gives up on you.

War

Bright lights and flashes light up the skies—
explosion, loud noises, and horrible cries.
Unknown reason for these acts—
men are dying and that is a fact.
Soldiers with their faces full of fear,
wondering if death is really near.
Why are we taking up arms?
Are we doing more good than harm,
having flown to a distant shore,
carrying bombs that already soar?
Oppression and tyranny have to go,
but one day war will cease, God said so.
Wars are fought to occupy land,
just like Russia, China, Korea, and Iran.
Fighting for oil, plutonium, diamonds, and gold,
many countries risk all they have, even their soul.
Mankind will always strive for more
and sometimes gets it by declaring war.
I pray we never open the door
and let the nuclear bombs soar

The Big Four

Three boys and one girl—
we were little children,
and to our mother
we were her whole world.
The four of us grew tall
in the same home,
learning and playing together,
never left alone.
Mom said we were to
always be real tight,
never let anything divide us,
to help one another even in a fight.
We learned rules that would
help us prosper and succeed:
work hard, be courteous, and loathe greed.
In our home honesty, fair play, and decency
were an absolute must.
They were the rules that
the big four had to trust—
family first, and we believe that still.

This was how we were raised.
We have our own children now,
and it's what we instill.
We are untied always,
come what may,
even though one brother
has now passed away.
We love all our family
and miss you more.
The love between us
will always endure,
and we will always be the big four.

Written for Pearline J. Woolfolk

White or Black

The world used to be white or black.
You were labeled, and that is a known fact.
This world is no longer so cut and dry.
It never was that way for you and I.
Really does make a difference where you were born.
If not rooted in America, then you're classified as foreign.
Many people have come across that border.
It does make a difference if your papers are in order.
The color of your skin and your accent too
made a difference for me, also for you.
I don't agree with everything black or white.
Be fair and don't discriminate or judge by sight.
Racism for many years has been under attack—

started with Lincoln, then Martin and Jack.
America will never be the land of the free.
It too has become enslaved by the wealthy.
I never thought I would see a time
when the president would have the
same color skin as mine.
We have been praying to God for a sign,
but every time we start to advance,
the powerful people say, "Don't give them a chance."
Now our brothers have come to sit at the table,
and the powerful say they are not able.
Powerful people don't cut anyone slack.
Wealthy people yearn for old days to come back,
when the whole world was white or black.
I love telling them it ain't never coming back!

Domestic Abuse

When love begins to abuse you,
then it's time to let it go.
Don't ever stay and take abuse.
Never go with the flow.
What will you have to gain
if your love causes bodily pain?
It should never bring about shame.
Love is for real, not an ugly game.
So many women have fear, and they have dread
that one day they will be found dead,
but still they stay and then forgive,
wondering how long they will continue to live.
We have to break this beast called abuse,
but until the people begin to rebel
they will continue to live in hell.
There is nothing good about abuse.

Drug Dealers

God has told me what to say,
so I'm writing to you today.
He has heard cries from on high
whose loved ones you have caused to die.
You sell drugs to people with weak minds
but leave death and destruction behind.
God said that you don't have too long.
You know what you're doing is wrong.
You heard it before, it's the same old song.
This is the message God told me to tell.
You can't sell drugs while you burn in hell.
Yes, that is where you are headed today.
You can't destroy lives and walk away.
There is definitely a price that you must pay.
It's not too late to change this view,
so listen, drug dealer, this is what you must do:
Fall on your knees, ask Jesus to enter your heart.
This is not the end but where you can start.

Find a church and read the Bible every day.
Don't forsake fellowship;
it will help along the way.
It's time for you to repent
and determine where your eternity
will be spent.

Everyman

In every man there is a gentle force,
a faithful beacon of light
that leads him on a righteous path
and through the darkest night.
In every man there is a tender song
to cheer him when he's blue,
a heartwarming melody of love
he always listens to.
In the heart of every man
there is a welcoming voice
that bids you to come into the light.
Let Jesus protect you from the evil night.
Jesus is the light, and he bids you to come in.
Only he can save your soul and forgive all sin.
You know the difference in wrong and right,
so come out of the darkness and into the light.

President Obama

President Obama, I pray for you
each and every night,
that you stay strong and
continue to fight.
Your first term you took it on the chin.
What a mess that you were left to defend.
At times you looked like Daniel in the lions' den.
Remember that circumstances can change.
I can see you are in a struggle,
trying to make things right—
not just for some Americans,
but all men red, black, and white.
We all know that you have been
under a fierce unending attack,
but stay strong and don't worry.
God has your back.
Your personal story inspires people
all over the world,
and you are loved by many
men, women, boys, and girls.
God chose you to bring
the world into the light,
appointed to do right.
I'll be praying again tonight.

Washington, DC

What's happening in DC?
Politicians are supposed to represent me,
but the congressmen that we sent
tried to shut down the government.
The rich people who don't even care,
still trying to stop our health care,
while many Americans go untreated
with illness and disease everywhere.
Serving the citizens and feeling their pain
have now diminished for personal gain.
Our country will never be the same.
We must have homegrown patriots again.
I hope we can come together as a nation.
Americans are tired of exploitation.
We need to be fair and just to all
or, like Rome, we'll burn and fall.

Mama Said

Mom told me long ago
life goes by fast
and only what you do
for God will last.
Don't ever forget your history,
but strive for what you want to be.
There will be tasks that have to be done.
Just never forget where you're from.
You come from a tribe that was strong
and also very bright—
tradesmen, teachers, and warriors
who never lost a fight.
No matter what you accomplish in life,
walk and stand tall in God's light.
Remember the lessons in the Bible.
Live by Jesus's word, and do what's right.
Lessons learned while you
were still very small
will one day make you stand
proud and tall.
You will soar higher than many
and lower than some.
Remember what Mama said,
and don't forget where you're from.

Mother's Day

Mother's Day means more than words
could ever say.
It's love remembered by you
and me in a very special way.
Many moms have gone on
to be with the king.
They are in his presence,
listening to the angels sing.
Yes, we miss our moms more
than words can ever say,
but they still live on inside of us
every single day.
God gave us a precious gift,
to love us while we grew.
That they would be gone so soon
we never knew.
They gave so much to
our families and friends.
The love that they gave lives on
in us and will never ever end.
So if your mother still lives today,
hug her really tight.
Tell her that you love her dearly,
'cause she will be going away one night.

Maya Angelou

Your voice will never be silenced.
Neither bright sunny days nor
cold rainy nights could ever quiet
the sound of your majestic voice.
It echoes across Southern fields
and heavily populated city streets.
It settles in tranquil villages, towns,
student-filled schools, and colleges.
On earth you were a poet, actress, singer,
activist. You danced and gained much fame.
Now, songbird, you have earned your wings
and are reciting for the king of kings.
Your earthly presence was not
in vain, because listening to you
the angels in heaven will know
why the caged bird sings.

Beautiful Lupita

I have never seen you before you hit the screen,
but I have seen your spirit in my dreams:
a beautiful black woman with poise and style.
Will you listen, Lupita, as I talk awhile?
During your time in the public eye,
stand tall and straight, and try not to cry.
Your journey has been longer than some,
but to be where you are many would die.
Don't get caught up in that Hollywood allure.
You are an African queen from the African shore.
Many men will want you because you are new
as the flavor of the year, and that is so true.
Deep dark chocolate and beautiful as can be,
I value all that you said and beamed with empathy.
Many of us understand the battle you fought,
and your victory over yourself wasn't for naught.
It's a battle many of us have come to detest.
Because of our skin shade we weren't as good as the rest—
a battle that still rages on each and every day,
with many wondering if it'll ever go away.
So, my beautiful queen, you are an icon,
and you have just begun your reign.
And Hollywood needs to take notice, as
you are going to be heard from again.

Dedicated to Lupita
Written by Larry Joseph

Muhammad Ali

That Muhammad Ali was the
greatest fighter of all time
no one could ever doubt.
I saw him knock many men out.
He was one of my heroes,
as you can see,
not just because of his boxing skills
but also his integrity.
Ali stood up for what
he believed was right,
while many other men
never even began to fight.
Ali never gave in to
insurmountable odds,
but the fight with the government
was not just his but also God's.
I love you, Ali, for the pride
you let me see,
the strength you exhibited,
and your integrity.

Loving You So

Whenever we quarrel
I have to stop and think
what happened to our love
to bring us to the brink.
There was a time when
our feelings would just flow,
and I couldn't help myself
from loving you so.
Time has gone by so very fast,
and now is the time to leave the past.
Just give in to my love so tender,
and finally let your heart surrender.
Your smile is like the morning sun
on a new day that has just begun.
Life has a way of coming around.
With me your true love can be found.
No matter what comes our way
I'll be there to spice up the day.
Just keep moving with our flow,
and I'll keep on loving you so.

Dedicated to Johnette G. Joseph

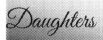

Daughters

When God blesses a man with a daughter
he beams with the pride that comes from inside.
It is such a wonderful feeling, one that he
just can't possibly hide.
Men don't realize love that will
change his whole world
until he has a little girl.
Love and respect, always protect,
handle her with care.
My love with my daughters
I will never share.
Fathers, you are the first man that
your daughters will ever love.
They think you are an angel
sent from above.
One day that little girl
will leave your protective world.
For sure you will be sad.
Letting go is hard for a dad,
nourish her to grow and mature;
Love, for you will forever endure.
Let your love shine like Jesus Christ,
love she will remember for the rest of her life.

Dedicated to Kelly and Vannisha

Message to My Son

Son, I love you, and no matter what comes your way I will be there for you. I was so proud when you were born and beamed with pride to see my son, a gift from God. Stay grounded in Jesus Christ, and remember to keep his commandments. The commandments are a guide for living and will lead to true happiness if you strive to embrace them.

In this life you will face adversity, but have no fear, for you have the innate ability to overcome every obstacle you are confronted with if you don't quit. There will be times when you may fall, but dust yourself off and get up and start over again. Don't give in to your fears, because they are just a thin veil that can be easily penetrated and you will walk through it. Don't give too much weight to the opinions of others, and keep your eye on Jesus at all times.

I'm your father, and as such I had to teach you right from wrong and make you accountable for your actions. Many traps have been set just to trip up young men and take away their most precious gift: freedom. I don't want you to fall prey to any of them. You have learned many lessons, and I have seen you mature as a young man, controlling both anger and rage.

You are a warrior and come from a long line of military men who fought for family and country in many wars of our great county. You too are a veteran, having now served your country honorably both stateside and on a distant shore.

Continue to maintain the highest level of self-respect and honesty, respecting the rights and property of others while allowing for the differences of opinions.

Pick your battles, my son, for there is a time to fight and there is a time for patience. Don't be led blindly into battle. Whenever possible choose your own battleground. Pray at all times, and ask God to direct your path.

Don't sweat the small stuff, my son. Save your energy for bigger battles; they are coming.

Stand tall and be proud of your heritage, and do nothing to stain it. Remember I love you, son, and will always be there for you. God has blessed you, and I add my blessings to his for wisdom and strength.

Dedicated to my son, Larry II

Get Off My Porch

What's the use in crying?
Because so many people are dying.
The establishment is still lying
while building more weapons to destroy the world.
Then when I speak the truth
God has placed in my mind,
you ask why am I tripping?
Just get off my porch.
We can't even stop the crime
but keep saying everything is fine.
But there are jobs that are never yours or mine.
What is the use in trying?
You don't believe the knowledge I'm giving you,
so you ask me again why I'm tripping.
But this ain't no trip; it's real life, but I'm tired.
Just get off my porch.
You need to think about the reason you ain't achieving
the goals you set in this life, regardless of the strife,
All that sweat, but you still in debt.
Haven't never seen success yet.

You can't figure this system out,
but you keep paying taxes and stay in debt.
Don't know what is happening with the government,
wondering how your tax money is being spent.
Now how you going to say I'm tripping?
At least I'm not grinning and skipping.
You have to stand up and be strong; it's no joke.
Get out and vote, help people to have hope.
I understand the government plan
made into law by the man,
but I have risen above the box in which they wanted me to stay,
because God showed me a better way.
Many great kingdoms tumble and fall.
Jesus and his kingdom outlast them all.
So I accepted Christ, and he showed me what to do.
Now I'm giving that knowledge to you.
So if you can feel what I'm telling you, it's good.
If not, get off my porch, and stop tripping.

Dedicated to my late brother, John Joseph Hampton (June Bug)

Summertime in Bristol

Hot and steamy with sweat dripping—
that good-tasting barbecue
that your tongue be licking
as you sway to the music of Marvin Gaye,
asking yourself why can't it
always be this way.
Family and friends getting it on
with the lyrics of a song,
your cousins trying to hide that bong,
babies crying, wanting to be held,
two guys hustling DVDs they trying to sell.
Big Mama said it was time to eat.
Some friends said the tea was just too sweet.
Now it's too hot, and everyone heading for the shade.
Some friends said he'll try the lemonade.
The ribs and chicken making a lot of smoke.
Now the men has started to tell his best joke.
Your pit bulls are starting to bark.
Better get the kids home; it's getting dark.
The dogs stop barking if you whistle;
that's the way you train them up in Bristol.
It's summertime, and all is good.
Every weekend we party and barbecue
until midnight in the hood … in the summertime.

Dedicated to my hometown, Bristol, Pennsylvania (The Terrace)

Brotherhood

The world needs brotherly love,
descending from heaven like a dove.
It doesn't matter where you go;
when men are united it will show.
Coming together from every race,
not even noticing time and space—
we need to find a better way.
All men are brothers, so kneel and pray.
Brotherhood lets the world see
peace developed through fraternity.
Decide now to love and do good.
A prime example is brotherhood.

Dedicated to my brother Lincoln Joseph III (L.J.)

The Big 4 Siblings Pearline, Bug, LJ, Larry

Larry Sr, and Larry II

Johnny Joseph Hampton

Ali

Johnette G. Joseph

Kelly & Vannisha

The Men

John, Lincoln, Larry, Dad

Johnny Joseph (Soldier)

Larry Senior

Thanks to my family for your love and support throughout the years: Pearlie M. Joseph, Lincoln Joseph II, Johnette G. Joseph, Vannisha P. Joseph, Larry Joseph II, Kelly and Scott Carrington family, John Hampton, Lincoln Joseph III, Pearline J. Woolfolk, Vannie Gregory, John L. and Doris Hills, Doc and Sarah Robinson, Bell Blake, Eula M. Mooks, Nan Carter, Boy and Margaret Carter, Blondie Canyon, Robert and Delores Hills, Ceola Cutliff, Denise Garrison, Rosalyn Blake, Sharon Fontenont, Douglas Woolfolk Jr., Rudine Cutliff, Jasper Cutliff, Mary Belton, Ruth Brown, Marvin Brown II, Kathryn Joseph, Johnny Joseph, Ruby Joseph, Benny and Margaret Joseph, Rosalyn and Eric Joseph, John Hills Jr., Kate Rice, Estelle Fralin, and Walt and Bert Williams, Ruth Morris, Thirththe Mcknight, Louise Nichols, Madison Joseph, Earl & Merriam Joseph.

Shout-Outs

Thanks for believing, Wayne White; Joe Caldwell; Robert Templeton; Johnny Morris; Les Jones; Spencer Singleton; Lutcher Wiltz II; Isaiah Adams; Albert and Margaret Gary; Algia Roseboro; Myrna Harris; Darlene Sexton; Paulette Hawthorne; Eunice Jackson; Doris and Rio Mobley; Deema Newberry; Billy and Patty Moore; Jimmy Reid; Dot Rogers; Alberta Howard; Ricky Wade; Deborah Davis; Donald Macky; Tony Fralin; Jimmy McHeny; Doug Malcom; Facebook family; Charlotte Observer family; Geneva, New York, family; and all my friends from Levittown, PA.; Bristol, PA.; St. Lucia; Jamaica; and the Bahamas, Harry Bosley, Jimmy McCoy.

New Waves Of Joy Baptist Church Family; Again, thank you.

Special Acknowledgment:

My friend and artist Albert Gary drew the illustrations of the angels, and Muhammad Ali. Albert also grew up in Bristol, Pennsylvania, and currently resides in Croydon, Pennsylvania. Thank you, Albert, for assisting me with your talent.

Printed in the United States
By Bookmasters